Luisa Rose
Wildblumen Kinder
Ausmalbuch für Erwachsene

Bibliografische Information der Deutschen Nationalbibliothek:
Die Deutsche Nationalbibliothek verzeichnet diese Publikation in der Deutschen Nationalbibliografie; detaillierte bibliografische Daten sind im Internet über http://dnb.dnb.de abrufbar.

© 2016 Luisa Rose; 1. Auflage
Covergrafik, Texte & Illustrationen © 2016 Luisa Rose

Herstellung und Verlag: BoD – Books on Demand, Norderstedt

ISBN: 9783743137707

SILVER ROD
[Solidago Bicolor]

Said Silver Rod, "My cousins all
Wear robes of gold the livelong Fall;
It's unbecoming to me 'ite,
And so I dress in crear ite.

DOWNY PHLOX
[*Phlox Pilosa*]

Said Downy Phlox, "Of all the West,
I love the rolling prairies best;"
Cousin Sweet William smiled and said,
"I like my own soft garden bed."

SHOWY GOLDEN ROD
(Solidago Speciosa)

"Our family is so large you see,"
  Said Showy Golden Rod to me,
"It keeps me nodding all the day
  To cousins who go by this way!"

LADY'S SORREL
[*Oxalis Cornucalate*]

Lady's Sorrel sleeps so tight
Throughout the peaceful summer night;
But her eyes fly open wide
When Sunbeam frolics by her side!

CLOSED GENTIAN
[*Gentiana Andrewsii*]

"O Bottle Gentian," begged the bees
"Open and give us honey, please?"
But Bottle Gentian shook his head,
"Belongs to Bumble Bee," he said.

HEPATICA
[*Hepatica Triloba*]

Hepatica comes bright and early,
Never tardy, never surly,
Wears a pretty lilac dress
And gives out joy and happiness.

INNOCENCE
[*Houstonia Caerulea*]

Innocence, the pretty thing,
Comes along in early Spring;
Wears sweet slips, the pretty pet,
In dainty shades of violet.

SHOOTING STAR
[*Dodecatheon Meadia*]

Said Shooting Star, "We're sure and steady,
And come as soon as we are ready;
We're not afraid of April's snows,
That's 'cause we're healthy, I suppose."

PASQUE FLOWER
[*Anemone Patens*]

Pasque Flower is a prairie child,
Doesn't wait 'till days are mild
But, wrapped in furs, she trips along
Before the Robin sings his song.

PAINTED TRILLIUM
[Trillium Undulatum]

Said Painted Trillium, "As you see
Our folks observe the rule of three;
The styles may change, but still we cling
To our tri-cornered hats each spring."

YELLOW STAR GRASS
[*Hypoxis Hirsuta*]

Yellow Star Grass hides in play
Among the grasses every day;
But when you call "I spy," she's fair;
Then you can find her anywhere!

SOLOMON'S SEAL
[*Polygonatum Biflorum*]

Solomon's Seal said, looking wise,
"Each may do something if he tries;
I feed the honey bees, the dears,
And keep a record of my years!"

MARSH MARIGOLD
[*Caltha Palustris*]

Marsh Marigold, bright cheerful thing,
Makes glad the days of early Spring;
She sprinkles gold stars one by one
That look like bits chipped from the sun.

PASTURE ROSE
[*Rosa Humilis*]

Said Pasture Rose, "The Bumble bee
Quite often leaves her babes with me;
I love to hold them next my heart;
I'm sorry when it's time to part!"

DAY FLOWER
[*Commelina Communis*]

Day Flower wears a gown of blue
That only lasts her one day through;
Her mother must be busy quite
To make a new one every night.

SHOWY LADY'S SLIPPER
[*Cypripedium Hirsutum*]

Showy Lady's Slipper knows
She's the prettiest thing that grows;
Her Orchid Cousins in the city
Say she's sweet as she is pretty.

SWEET WHITE VIOLET
[*Viola Pallens*]

Sweet White Violet came to bring
To us the fragrance of the Spring;
Dearest maid in all the wood,
Sweet and modest as she's good.

RED CLOVER
[*Trifolium Pratense*]

Red Clover swaying in the breeze
Holds receptions for the bees;
Doesn't care for sweets himself
But likes to feed each hungry elf.

FROSTWEED
[*Helianthemum Canadense*]

Frostweed's sometimes called Rock Rose,
He doesn't mind how cold it grows;
Laughs, and thinks it's rather nice
To trim his cap with bits of ice.

JEWELWEED
[*Impatiens Biflora*]

"Beware of me," said Jewel Weed,
"I'm very dangerous, indeed;"
  But still the fairies wouldn't stop,
  They teased him just to hear him "pop."

COMMON MALLOW
[*Malva Rotundifolia*]

Little Common Mallow said,
"I could not live inside a bed;
I like to roam just where I please;
The little children play I'm cheese!"

ROSE MALLOW
[*Hibiscus Moschentos*]

Rose Mallow is a happy child,
She likes damp places, in the wild;
Blooms nearly all the summer through
To make a lovely world for you.

GOLD THREAD
[*Ceptis Trifolia*]

Perhaps in woodland walks you've seen
Sir Gold Thread dressed in evergreen;
They say the gnomes and fairies use
His roots of gold to lace their shoes!

MONKEY FLOWER
[*Mimulus Ringens*]

Young Monkey Flower put up a sign;
"Keep Out! This honey is all mine!"
But Bumble Bee just went ahead,
"I'm sure that don't mean me," he said.

HEAL ALL
[*Prunella Vulgaris*]

Heal All wears a purple bonnet
With some dainty colors on it;
Sometimes brightens her green clothes
With tiny bits of purple bows.

JOB'S TEARS OR, SPIDERWORT
[*Tradescantia Virginiana*]

Job's Tears is such a funny lad!
He weeps all day! He isn't sad;
Just got the habit! All the season
He weeps for neither rhyme nor reason.

CATNIP
[Nepeta Cataria]

Old Dr. Catnip's glad to call
On pussies big and pussies small;
But says, "If you'll all come to me
I'll make you well without a fee."

ST. JOHN'S WORT
[*Hypericum Perforatum*]

Common St. John's Wort is a tramp,
But he's a jolly little scamp;
Scatters his bloom along the way
Like golden coins his way to pay.

TWIN FLOWER
[*Linnaea Borealis Americana*]

Twin Flower Children, dainty pair,
Sprinkle fragrance on the air;
Seldom, elsewhere will you meet
Flower Children half so sweet.

BELL FLOWER
[Campanula Rapunculoides]

Little Bell Flower ran away
From the gardener one fine day,
Never did come back again;
Liked it better on the plain!

STAR-FLOWER
[*Trientalis Americana*]

Dainty Star-Flower seemed to say,
As I raced through the woodland way;
"Don't be afraid, I'll give you light,
Just as the sky-stars do at night!"

BLUE SPRING DAISY
[*Erigeron Pulchellas*]

Blue Spring Daisy said, "I'm chilly
In my lavender gown so frilly
If I try to bloom too soon,
And so I wait till May or June."

COMMON BUTTERCUP
[Ranunculus Acris]

Little Common Buttercup,
If you'll hold her gently up
To your dimpled chin, will tell
If you love butter very well.

FALSE LILY OF THE VALLEY
[*Maianthemum Canadense*]

False Lily of the Valley said,
"I'll choose another name instead;
Canada Mayflower it shall be;
There's nothing false, sir, about me."

BELLWORT
[*Uvularia Perfoliata*]

If through the woods you'll walk in May
You'll see the Bellwort children play
At hide and seek, in yellow coats
With their wee cousins, sweet Wild Oats.

Weitere Ausmalbücher von Luisa Rose:

Titel	ISBN
Alice im Wunderland	9783741297502
Blumen und Märchen	9783743102002
Der Struwwelpeter	9783743102699
Die Struwwelliese	9783743102811
Don Quixote	9783743104037
Drei kleine Schweine	9783743104099
Eine Blumenhochzeit	9783743104105
Fröhliche Reigenspiele	9783743104112
Lustige Tanzspiele	9783743104273
Reise ins antike Griechenland	9783743112568
Flucht ins antike Griechenland	9783743112599
Pariser Leben im 19.Jahrhundert	9783743112704
Die Sommerkönigin	9783743112742
Der Schneider und die Krähe	9783743112827
Die Wikinger	9783743113275
Hänsel und Gretel	9783743114265
Max und Moritz	9783743103214
Schnurrdirburr	9783743112834
Mode des 18. und 19. Jahrhunderts	9783743112971
Kostümbilder des 18. und 19. Jahrhunderts	9783743114401
Abenteuer im Bienenland	9783743117051
Griechische Helden der Antike	9783743117709
Märchen alter Zeit	9783743116559
Wildblumen Kinder	9783743137707
Blumenfeen	9783743137738

Notizbücher von Luisa Rose:

Titel	ISBN
Drachentöter (Notizbuch)	9783743113077
Natures Wonders (Notizbuch)	9783743113817
Gedankenspiel Notizen (Notizbuch)	9783743113886
Smaragd Notizen (Notizbuch)	9783743114296
Jagd Notizen (Notizbuch)	9783743114302
Tradition (Notizbuch)	9783743114319
Antik Notizbuch (Notizbuch)	9783743114326
Veni Vidi Vici (Notizbuch)	9783743114340
Black List (Notizbuch)	9783743114371
Mystic Notes (Notizbuch)	9783743114388
Magic Notes (Notizbuch)	9783743114418
Fantasien (Notizbuch)	9783743114463
Creative Notes (Notizbuch)	9783743114487
Persönliche Notizen (Notizbuch)	9783743114494
Peter Pan (Notizbuch)	9783743114531
Rose (Notizbuch)	9783743114548
Quality Street (Notizbuch)	9783743114555
Rubin Notizen (Notizbuch)	9783743114647
Schmetterlinge (Notizbuch)	9783743114661
Ali Baba (Notizbuch)	9783743114678
The portrait of a Lady (Notizbuch)	9783743114692
Shakespeare (Notizbuch)	9783743114722
Brainstorming (Notizbuch)	9783743114739
Merlin (Notizbuch)	9783743114746
Rügen (Notizbuch)	9783743114784

Möchtest du über neue Bücher von Luisa Rose per email Informiert werden? Dann schicke eine Email mit ‚Newsletter' im Betreff an Luisa.Rose@t-online.de